# MAN READING
# "WOMAN READING IN BATH"

Also by John Livingstone Clark

## Poetry

*Poems From a Broken Body* (Saskatoon: Thistledown Press, 2005)

*Body and Soul: Poems New and Selected* (Toronto: Exile Editions, 2002)

*Stream Under Flight* (Saskatoon: Thistledown Press, 1999)

*Passage to Indigo* (Toronto: Exile Editions, 1996)

*Prayers and Other Unfinished Letters* (Toronto: Exile Editions, 1995)

*Breakfast of the Magi* (Saskatoon: Thistledown Press, 1994)

*Stepping up to the Station* (Regina: Coteau Books, 1990)

*Towards 2000: Poetry for the Future* (anthology, with Martha Gould)
(Saskatoon: Fifth House, 1991)

## Prose

*Back to Bethany: 89 Paragraphs About Jesus and Lazarus in Abbotsford*
(Toronto: Exile Editions, 1997)

# MAN READING
# "WOMAN READING IN BATH"

JOHN LIVINGSTONE
CLARK

thistledown press

Thistledown Press Ltd.
633 Main Street
Saskatoon, Saskatchewan, S7H 0J8
www.thistledownpress.com

Library and Archives Canada Cataloguing in Publication

Clark, R. J. (Ronald John), 1950-
Man reading "Woman reading in bath" / John Livingstone Clark.

Poems and ghazals.
ISBN 978-1-897235-59-1

1. Szumigalski, Anne, 1922- . Woman reading in bath. 2. Ghazals, Canadian.
I. Title.

PS8555.L37185 M35 2009 C811'.54 C2009-900759-2

Cover photograph (detail): **Tom Morrison/Getty Images:**
Cover and book design by Jackie Forrie
Printed and bound in Canada

10 9 8 7 6 5 4 3 2 1

Thistledown Press gratefully acknowledges the financial assistance of the Canada Council for the Arts, the Saskatchewan Arts Board, and the Government of Canada through the Book Publishing Industry Development Program for its publishing program.

To my much loved friend and mentor, Anne Szumigalski, who helped me realize my deepest dream, and to Lorna Crozier, whose gorgeous book of ghazals, *Bones In Their Wings: Ghazals* (Hagios Press) reawakened my fascination with that exotic form.

# Contents

# 1/

# Faltering Ghazals

1.

flat square stones in lush green turf—
how many names forgotten?

marriage bands white aflutter—purple
petals—wind in lilacs—

one knee gone—you kneel every day
for the promise of night—

grandfathers dead with missing fingers—
people forgotten—

the first crocus—then tulips—then
fiery tiger lilies—

five pairs of highly arched eyes—a
cathedral/ surprised—

squat green dumpsters—enough empties
you think/ for morning communion—

blunt rusty blade—who dares to doubt
an axe? the wind does—

2.

lilies and tulips where least expected—an
old broken man leaves home—

a garbage truck's clatter and horn—but un-
derneath and distant/ cathedral bells—

a dancer's slender leg—a steeple's narrow
grace—both rising—

brick turned a sandy salmon hue—this
church that can't spawn—

not red or brown—but much dust and many
tears to make a single brick—

swift summer rivers—snowmelt and cool—
now prairie mouths open—

stone arched windows—hands held in prayer—
god or not—how spires reach—

3.

old electric fans breathe heavy with the
heat—a tentative love expires—

lobster claws for the holy ghost—as the old
and lame push forward with walkers—

truth or illusion—bread and wine—
the dance of varying altars—

backs sore from wooden pews—piano benches
no better—beauty's unnatural gaze—

words and burning tongues—only caraganas
listen to the light—

the cripple with his pallet sits beside
a stream of color—

a boy down from the mountain—fire
and water—who is a friend?

## 4.

brass funeral urn on baby
car-seat—don't think—

pixies and dragonflies—
mind and world—

sea and sky—why hydrogen
plays like a god—

red and white capsules—the
friendliest of doors—

a cedar and fir soul/scape—
no life without trees—

crazy people standing still and
mute—always scene stealers—

alders and aspens edging dirt roads—
plain and simple—

a pieta carved from pine—the up/
turned roots a grotto—

5.

cathedrals can't blow over
like potted shrubs—

the living become ghosts when
their hearts wander off—

diamond shapes on shingled roof—
house that would be a lotus—

still brown water—tadpoles dead—
who makes the rules?

desert or beach—coyotes or crabs—
any meal a communion—

moving house and dying both
require time—

6.

arms  legs  trunk  head—you grow
from birth into a cross—

woman with sex-doll mouth—man
with a hard rubber mind—

passion fruit and flowers—every
kiss sweetly decays—

any pupil can learn to be a mirror—
apple seeds or basalt—

you move painfully to a natural out-
side—where winter moons bleed—

'personality' a hat too big—with the
brim over eyes/  sight unseen—

saying goodbye/  the mind leaves
—a mist on the ground—

7.

pressure sores that never heal—scabs
at a beggar's banquet—

beauty at the window sill—daisies
and lilies almost still—

how many lovers to suicide? even
bouquets insufficient—

a taste of lips eyelids tongues—
the honeybee's nectar—

you forget if they're used for the living
or dead—prayers and unbidden love—

pale orange beaches in the south pacific—
my 'ozzie' lover an hourglass—

tiger lilies like a mind's last thought—who
knows where beauty travels?

8.

supple boughs and limbs—weightless
on a dancing wind—

too soon the cross rises through fading
flesh—femurs over spine—

cathedrals in the shadow of life's brief
bubble—altars that never were—

the fear of words ending/  light dimming—
the heart's broken silk—

children  lovers  friends—webs in
a forest—

behind your navel the lapping of waves—
there you'll board a darkened ship—

9.

a skull full of azure—the grim
smile absorbed—

moths on a summer breeze like
friends called to a wake—

black/tulips  white/roses— echoes
of laughter in a red vase

sparrows tear through a spider's web—
chaos and rain—

people undone by a lack of doing:
arms  legs  hands  minds—

dream of a time when dreaming will stop—
fishing boats moored at fulford harbour

10.

an eldest son brings you gifts of life—
pansies  ferns  tiger-lilies—

giving plants water he pulls out a Buddha—
both smile when wet—

forest ferns behind streaked jade—hues
of green—a fat round belly—

too many words can strangle the heart—
better giving and being—

baptisms  weddings  funerals—the church
next door/  an empty train station—

saint james and a gospel of doing the
'love'—right action opens all—

water plants/ Buddha dust—but no
one comes here anymore—

11.

april / big blades clear streets of dirty
snow:  veins and arteries

show a way to the heart—the jugular/
for example/  is not a fool—

when walking in the face of death/
leave a trail of coloured rocks—

breadcrumbs soon devoured
by rats and stoats—

in july the chlorophyll leaves no one
feeling empty—a god should be green—

on hands and knees people rejoice
family /  sniffing  sighing—

in a snap of time's fingers/  we come
and go—we grow like weeds—

## 12

in a wilderness/  no ears to hear
thunder—no eyes for lightning—

imagination goes everywhere mind
can't:  moth over butterfly—

tons of red brick to build a cathedral—
how does *pneuma* ever get through?

spiderwebs  lacy ferns—both sentient beings—
breeze through a window—

roses whiter then bone china—love still
sweeter than death—who has a choice?

everything living seeks an earthen embrace—
sparrows and swallows fly into glass—

13.

hands you've never let go of—ropes and
chains not felt before—

why a sense of wind under wings?  this
song can't be yours—

bleed like an inverted lamb—bleating
will not move the stone—

soul departed—what sloshes as if
from a broken cask?

emptiness like a palpable brook—
nothingness a flood—

lost beneath white water and rocks—
your everyday self—

ball/gloves  hats  lawn/mowers and rakes—
the welcoming smile gone—

14.

couplets but no coupling—funereal con/
junctions—the garden dead—

a drop of mercury on a silent tongue—
suddenly words hover—

a mind co/equal with cosmos—what
makes it sometimes so—

a union of opposites—opiates and
apples/  snakes and larks—

love songs tumble down hollow legs—
extremities too extreme—

snakes amongst the robins' eggs—
who knows when it ends?

when a building burns and there are no
exits—swallow yourself alive—

15.

living forward into future—we die
backwards into time—

eleven steps down a spiral stair/
case—a large oaken door

a rough stone chamber—
quite small/ when it opens/

modern life disappears—then
suddenly rocky crags of snow and scree—

river valleys embracing the plains—
the heart quickly broken

a rosy/mauve dawn
through blue/bottle glass—this hoax

now come to an end—light
motes with hope of rising—

## 16.

step out on a branch
to find the tree—

climb high up the limbs—
to find roots—dig deep

follow the tendrils to find fruit—
apples in a light green sky—

is the face in the window at night
your own?

that visage could be anyone—self/
reflection

reflection demands dark
as well as light—

every window needs
the night

to become a mirror—stay
up late—watch trees grow—

17.

black crows on cathedral's
silver roof—not a cloud

in the sky—debussy
ebbs in and out

noisy fans—too
much humid heat—

in smithers/ bc/ you'd be
in a bar right now—

drink to the local glacier—
and the cool lake

in fulford harbour right now
you'd be ashes in the ground—

in vancouver, you'd be sitting
on the cliffs at ubc—

georgia strait/ snow capped peaks
small islands   your family—

here / day and night/
too far from the ocean

18.

there is Buddha's transcending
of all desire—

the heart crushed / mortar
and pestle—

in both cases *eros* loses—and
blood clots

between marble and stone—
without some small fire

a torch / we walk
backwards into

a sanguinary sea—cold sun
setting

a blade cuts into the wrist—the sky
suddenly full of poppies—

19.

smooth cold fingers caress your
face—a small oak covered with vines—

morning glory and death/ the showy
white blossoms

fanfare for leaving—who knows
where the vines root?

when do tendrils start to climb? that
genus of adversity—

## 20.

as if winter were to last
all year—some lives are too long—

maple leaves/ sodden brown
and red—folded with frost—

what loses shape does sometimes lose
the will to be—

rotting teeth /crumbling bone/
time crawls

as if there were only one leaf on a tree
only one tree in a forest

21.

no need for stone or bone
vase—the flowers have withered—

apologize to your body for such neglect—
you were not without water in this life—

staring into the sun
as foolish as flying too close—

the height you fall from/
where your body lands

22.

your children being born—
terror / wonder and so much blood—

a boy behind an old cedar shack / black
berries / wild roses—

before the eyes of a dying man /
poems appear from behind the moon

thick brambles surround the old
wire gate—no exit here

23.

small plump hands and limbs—
fingers fragile to the touch—

your arms a cradle/ your love
a citadel

among lilac scented sleepers—
woollens to hold the heat—

your heart achieves
*rubedo* / it endures—

24.

pearl grey sky above—limned
with pale cold light—

broken strains of music over
a silver tidal plain—

a slow piano movement—ravel
or debussy—

riding the breezes like a
small feathered kite—

or maybe something gaelic/
*breisleach* or *aodann*—

deep trench in your mind—
whose will be done?

25.

old pier/ grey weathered planks
and pilings—where was the cafe?

the back bedroom you knew as a child—
put down for naps

soft sea rhythms below / brine
against rock footings—

gulls and eagles—age four—
wonder and worry

hanging on the offshore wind—
time and time again

you return—enough is enough—
and rise like a kite—

2/

# Man Reading
# “Woman Reading In Bath”

## Man Reading Woman

### Part A

she says and says again  'I cannot get beyond this
enveloping darkness . . . this movement of arms and
shoulders in choppy cold brine  and how long ago
did the sun set?  several years perhaps?  time
so mysterious with
    its absence of markers—

first you're a child  flowers land in your hair
birds flutter in the air before your eyes—
    then child becomes woman or man
    hot living blood  sharp and lethal
    or slow like rhizomes
    and the orchids of spring—

earth/fire changes and woman becomes mother
        man becomes father—
then blossoming light    and lesions appear
in the lining of that inner cosmos—
                something squirms through
and where once there was only a whisper
of shadow   see now a single arc:
        child  adult  parent  grandparent—
all within and gradually
                        numinous:

                ashes in an old blue tobacco tin—

Part B

but always there is the child—picking blossoms
and thorns from long ashen-locks—or grown
in spirit    picking paths through august bush
        like thistle willow and rowan still young—
        eye of babe / tongue of youth
                twisted hands / back of crone—
through order and disorder who follows whom?

I haven't seen a mirror for years    the moon
hasn't shone on the sea for months—
                    but a yearning for eternity
                    rises in the waves we are:
and always the question
        Who is swimming?  stroke  after stroke—
                aorta pumping its own
                        sanguinary cheer—

blood/ocean  artery/river  vein/creek

limbs now much older  but the heart so
young that blackness
                no longer terrifies—
who would think that such depths
    and heights could be comforting?
on my back—hands slowly sculling—I swim
    between worlds  my invocations
          of loss crying up to the vault—
thin points of light like silver nibs
     in a coal-black sky  words
          taking shape
               in the translucent rain

## "I Am Swimming Alone On A Dark Sea"

*I swim   I have swum   I will be swimming*
always there will be swimming and I dream
of 'manta ray'
        gliding seas with great wings
        flapping here and there at salmon
                        snapper  flounder cod
cracking my tail like a bull whip—

I have never been a man / I think   have
never endured the complexities
                        of legs and feet—
    honestly   was I ever a man?

dreaming of furloughs on cobbled lanes?
        swimming has clouded the
        terran edges . . . the horizon's a line
        never at rest:
                        O sea swell . . . O tidal pull . . .

## The Her/Man Gaze

once a man gazed from plate-glass windows
with royal blue drapes:
        pleat   beyond fold   over ridge—
these proto/pelagic curtains seemed
        almost timeless
                        horizontal / unending
in the aesthetic of their hanging—

looking at scarlet berries   he saw salmon eggs
exploding with life—shining silver missiles
delicate jaws
        sharp teeth like the nibs of fountain pens—

*Tidal pull / cold ocean swell* he murmured /
*receive this offering—*
        steel-blue waves white capped   swelling
                a pristine life in broadening seas:
                        dreams of healing and words

## Short Snippits for Red Snappers

I.

I would have preferred
the webbed toes I was born with;

I would also have kept
the scarlet gills and salamander tail.

II.

en/dolphins: a chemical found in the brain/ creating sensations
of conscious swimming/ : the mind 'afloat,' so to speak.

## The Distance of Measure

do we all swim alone on the same dark sea?
no one's in sight/
                    no one's in hailing range—
          *but sometimes there is/*
                    *a sense of being seen—*
long distance swimmers, for example,
always have an escort   small vessels
          full of well-wishers   coaches

but no escort for us   our kind allergic
          to the new millennium
          (its dedication to golden calves
                    with silver spoons)—
try sleeping   but nothing changes
          when you close your eyes   still
          the heart pumps out its own
                              encouragement—

first was search and then despair
          but now there is only rhythm
                              direction immaterial:
          the wild currents under the body

## “ . . . Alone . . . ”

*long smooth strokes pull you into the surf* . . . Ozzie crawl /
breast stroke—you swim for twenty minutes   then stand up
looking back—how shallow this bay is   miles from shore
                    the surf only up to your chest—

but no hurry for depth   not with such a long way to go—
your two sons wrestling in the surf   have children of their own—
your daughter looks out to sea and waves   you are sure
she's smiling . . . even when in pain—

at the bay's mouth   deep currents pull you quickly from shore
the water changing colour—blue becomes sea-green—then
black-as-night under foam luminescence—
        covering arms shoulders—you pretend to be Poseidon
        but your hair stinks of dead-fish   plankton   kelp
        calling power from beyond birth   you pray quietly
        with each stroke—*out here*
                    *a cross would float*

## Water Wings Do No A Butterfly Make

what do I know of dying?   get up every morning
have breakfast   attend to the body—
a tune plays on the radio—
a simple piano piece    Satie perhaps
odd chords strung together
in different centuries—
then into my day    a dream of watery death
the open sea  coming for its own—
the prodigal body reclaiming its soul?

what's to be learnt by sinking to these depths?
the innate holiness of distance    as Aldous H.
taught        depth is simply distance /  and
the 'gravitas' of going straight down—

## Once You Had A House

but now it's the swim/zone for us   and I'm stroking towards you
over a black silent sea—though maybe it's just wishful thinking:
        "when you get that job at the library downtown you'll
        have to stay with me in the winter—of course you can't
        be driving out of town
                        on those blizzardy nights".

but you never made it to winter—went swimming instead . . .
dreaming of a play to perform in spas/ ponds/ pools
all across europe—
        you would be queen of mermaids . . . and I would be
        a simple pool boy with a long-handled brush—I
        don't know how your version went    but I dreamt
        that in the final act   I fell into the pool . . .
                        then swam up your sacred tunnel—

was I making love to the mermaid queen?   it started as something
erotic . . . but once in the vaginal cave volcanoes erupted . . . desire
more than furnace heat we meet in loins   and everywhere
a brilliant light   coloured as if stars bursting in a dark
primordial cave   how could a woman—a mermaid
queen—have so much room in her womb?

*perhaps she's an egg of infinity*, I mused   a cosmic
portal with arms and legs—
you once had a house   but now you're swimming far ahead
across a dark light of cavernous silence—

## . . . The Dark Sea

I was swimming—
now I'm floating on my back—
waves carry me where they will
gentle swell and bobbing
like father
in a WW2 Corvette—

any further north
they'd be chipping
ice off my rigging—

but this latitude suffices:
pineapples float by
pursued by giant
sea-turtles—
I have all the latitude I need

## . . . Dark

a manatee swam across my path—gentle sage —
and I'd seen pictures before so knew
a single long braid
streamed from behind her head—
the creature turned to me with huge blue eyes
encoding—*you seem quite tired . . . why not hang*
*on and I'll take you for a ride*—
so I grabbed the braid turned to where
she was going and soon I was skimming
along at fantastic speed—

pulling myself up to her head I asked politely
where her ears might be—*ears* she imaged
*I have no need of ears . . .*
*everything in water knows everything else*—
*you don't need speech . . . water always rises*
*to its own level of comprehension*—
but where are we going?
where are you going?
questions poured from my mouth—or seemed to—
did my lips even move? *you have no need to know*—
and I closed my eyes
mind turning to water

## "I Am Swimming . . . "

says the water in my bones    says the water
in my blood brain eyes liver—
        I am swimming alone in this man
        who thinks he's swimming alone on the sea—
        which thinks it's alone on all this earth
        which spins through the heavens
                        abhorring isolation—
I am the loneliest entity in all existence
says every entity in existence—and
        there is nothing so foolish as man
        splashing alone—though at some point
                the shadow overtakes the body

## Novalis Says That For Every Illness There Is A song To Cure It—

I have listened long and hard to waves sounding on the beach
I have listened closely on three continents—
                    but I know that in illness there
                    will be no music to heal me    though
                    I have lived music my entire life:
Gaelic music / bagpipes
teaching me to swim    to breathe underwater...
        or the enormity of Bach
        whose world taught me to let go of things
              on riverbanks and shoreline—
        boats run aground, girls, wives—
              roots of old trees    big cottonwoods—
jazz gave release    the great Coltrane
of consciousness . . . every possible nuance
stored away in the brain
              flowing down to the fingertips—
              a leap of . . . what?
diving forward into something new
              like water / not water—
        then breast stroke or butterfly   arms
        shoulders   quietly thrusting—
                    Zawinul's  'in a silent way'

## In Winter the Sun Travels Low Across the Sky

skimming horizons like a flying fish
air whistles through diaphanous wings—
                    like oboes
                    in a new-music quartet—
there is no order to the scales
no sea-currents pulling me like orange
peel   or bits of banana palm
          across the seas to Gauguin's grave
                    or Basho's Japan—

but these are only old visions
left behind like kindling
                    on a long midnight beach—
                              why ever be cold?

## "Under the Square Shadow of His Shoulders He Heaves Up on Stick Legs Like A Fat Bird"

'Nobodaddy' . . . what ever gave him the notion
he could walk? or carry himself erect like that?
hauling stone tablets—
leading tribes hither and yon—
the idea of it . . . in a world of water
in a universe shaped for floating—

having remade himself in the
image of primates—
a one and only god?
what a dangerous thing for everyone
no wonder his bones
became brittle so fast—there is
never enough milk
for a One and Only God—

## "Why Water In So Many Titles"?

she said one day . . .

a rhetorical question?   a meditation?

because water's closer to our true origins—

I throw myself into another wave . . . the tossing

sea at sunset   fiery brine

spume of white at blue hem—

but in black calm . . . her voice,

*I am swimming*

on a dark sea—

I would go to her   if there was a way—

## In the Arms of A Rowan I Float in Deeper Stillness

too much swimming and even the sea becomes confused—
who am I trying to impress this far from shore?

all minds dissolved by the bite of infinite brine—

so I take a small leafless tree in my arms . . . and
with arms / legs in motion—lift limbs in rhythm
                                        to the lyric waves—

I understand completely—the way
    of a timeless zone is both wet and dry—
                    the weather of transformation—

## 'Nobodaddy' Meets His End

### Part/1

anorexic god/wraith
this mumbling gnosis
tumbles and breaks bones—
        like any hoary old man
his beard hides a
multitude of flaws—

but this one sought to be God
the One God:
chased primary couplers
from paradise . . . put rocks
on the necks of the dying—
   calling it righteous—
law before love
          justice before mercy
                   retribution
          before anything happens—
sudsy water in the crone's bath
and he rose up  challenging
women one too many times—
too many commandments
his beard strangling everyone—

Part/2

finally . . . down he goes
and now at last . . . Justice
Eve no longer the 'weaker vessel'—
                    for stories change
          with author and editor—
the woman freed   she sprouts
fins/ gills/ saw-teeth
 pineal gland    then
says    I seem to be swimming
          alone in a sea—
a memory of apples and
a man named Adam
a vision of flaming swords
of angry beardless men in
nightshirts and halos—
driven from home . . .
                    the garden still in season—

Part/3

now swimming is so natural . . . and if
the crone  wants apples
                    she imagines an island—

if Adam wants to sire races . . .
he'll either learn to swim
                    or stay soft and dry—
          estranged
from Mother's bounty . . .

                    to be born   the water
                                        must break

## "Oh What A Dry and Brittle Skeleton He Makes"

but so easy to throw stones    made in his image I can swim as far
as I want and still—there it is—that comb of ribs

imperfect image of imperfect god    when you collapsed in the bath
we all cheered . . . shuddering in our sticks and bones

there but for the grace of who?    and in cold dark . . . when all I
want to do is sink into the grace
                                        of whom ever calls out—
(Pleroma
        the crone said
                                        and I have felt that fullness)

what I feel now is the weight of bones
                                                that is time come calling

                                        oh let me sleep

## Picture Yourself

on a seabed flat as a dinner plate   and about the same size
the sea looks strange and frightening . . . then you realize that
both your eyes are on the same side of your body   the top
side—in short you have become a flounder

nothing like this was ever in the cards . . . though the crone had
much advice and many warnings   but nothing to counter this—
a safety test of some kind, perhaps?   Okeanos seeing what I'm
really made of?  try crossing the abyss   that void of infinite
absence—try crossing as a flounder   then I'll know
                                                  how serious you really are—

# Tendrils From A Beard

naturally   they'd come from you   who else so determined
so bad tempered   always having to have his way—angels in
your beard their light diminished   but preening and grooming
dead stars from your grey coiling tendrils—

anointing with honey the father of all Be/es . . . *let it be/ let it be*
the angels sing   working their long fingers down to beard roots
wings like hummingbirds   they fly to your ears to trim black
wires drooping over your lobes—

without wife to keep you . . . without Sophia/wisdom . . . the tendrils
fall everywhere into our world:  omnipotent?   disrupting all daily
discourse . . . children thrown from horses   then frightened on high
altars . . .   boys reduced to radioactive dust   women to mules

but the old crone swims to her own rhythm . . . won't hear the beat
   of your priestly drum—and she asserts
            "man's best friend has never been dogma"—

## Going

to your grave to pray
waves lap over the seawall
gulls sweep over the shore
driftwood piled
like pale corpses—
the enemy within / the enemy without—
the enemy in uniform
invisible to the eye

discernment is learned
at sea . . . is earned in crossing
from drowning to lyfe
and rising to naught—
the enemy / is not nothing—

even drowning to naught
and rising to lyfe

## "Crack Crack the Shanks Have Snapped And Down He Flops On the Shingles Gasping and Stranded"

old before his time    we thought him eternal but look at the
wrinkles
the sagging tits    black heads just above beard:   didn't anyone
have time to clip his hair    in ears and nose?

I thought I was going to be strong for ever / he muttered   how I
made
them tremble in olden times . . . floods  fiery bracken  towns
aflame

then his chin hit the sand—milky eyes fluttering—lips moving
but uttering no speech    just moans groans and the sounds of a
heavenly chorus . . . every rib breaking like a city losing its walls
and foundations   houses/palaces/armouries   hear the crunch
of pelvis and vertebrae   markets/arenas . . . even temples
collapsing by the thousands

# A Trick With Lips and Tongue

1.

a small puff of air   a pull at the throat—
trick of tongue and lips—

grace notes sewing shut a world
'nobodaddy'   sundered
poems   stitches   spells
in search of vocation—
poetry
an invocation

2.

a simple pot   lead/lined as any roman
would have it—three
figures fashioned on the sides—

bull, lion, eagle—a fourth
unclear . . . then descent   a fire
searing blade bright
though nothing as simple as angels—
heralds of a god revealed

3.

to fall into depth of *Psyche* . . . wavelets
encoding like abalone—
a tempered ringing—
inner ear  the navigator
and wake with sea birds
crying  diving  wheeling—

the stiff winds cold  comfortless at
dawn—but still
the new light
breaking through—

## A Woman's Body Needs Open Water

false gods come apart    stone tablets dissolve like bromide—and
stern tenets follow—but a woman's body in bath is a rich coral
reef . . . feeding off and being fed upon    everything around it
paying court:
        wolf eel    manta ray    tiger shark    barracuda—

an endless list of ranks and orders—angel fish    star fish
sun fish    sea horse—the stones beneath pale feet redolent
of a distant ocean    where beaches were cold and grey like
slate—but where water made her skin tingle    like a blithe
        effervescence    and beneath gun metal
        waves were shells never before inhabited:
        as if God had been interrupted—

the girl—however—had made sea/snails from marzipan
placing them in the vacuous whorls    and at the end of
her labour she said a short prayer from the Gospel of Tom—

but the snails disappeared very quickly    altering in no way the
saline level—which is why this woman needs to soak . . . calling
up from the depths

## In the Fullness Of the Swim

mid-stroke / suddenly / a vision of you naked on your side—curling
up foetal like / dying    forsaking the quest for what Id
                                        and Persona most desire—

I don't know who you are    but tissues exude the fear of death—
like greasy blood from a wingless bird—are you as tired
as I was    at the end of my baptism?    contrition
in the deepest cavities of flesh?

yet there you are in the midst of my day—seeking prayer
like a crushed black moth    staining an altar—rolling
over naked from one last tryst—one last cry
                                        of the body's craving—

# He Swims . . .

a shark has taken a piece of spine
a small nibble from vertebrae six
now he bobs with frozen limbs
hands / fingers / toes / numb—
in lower torso a terrible pressure . . .

rolling onto his back   he feels guilty
about a lack of progress—is anyone
keeping track of distance?  is God?

if he could disbelieve in God   then
there would only be time—he could
travel looking up   softly sculling his
big toes   lifting
                    sea / spume to the stars—

## Under Summer Stars . . . Above the Irish Sea

off the coast of northern Wales   I floated for days
while you sang the songs of your childhood—the songs
of a four-year-old girl:
*wild/flowers   knights and maids   spells for good*
but now words don't matter:
                                        just breathing and silence—
and for luck the proximity
                                        of starfish and angelfish—
          *in the beginning was the word*
                                        but before then was the abyss—
          then the sky beyond sky
where a bowl of first fruits
          issued *Gaia / Okeanos*   earth and sea:
          to span the dimension
                    for a four year old's dreams—

## We See the Sun

stroke   stroke   stroke—haven't seen the crone now for two
months—last appearance:   sitting astride a giant sea turtle
throwing Sofia to the wind—
        Mr. B says "*the body is the emanation of the spirit*"
        then   smiling broadly   they dove quickly out of sight . . .

but am I tired—nothing much to rest on for days: a whale shark
short-sighted luckily—then a mahogany log:
        *but there are rules when one is seeking—when one seeks/*
        *one swims*—the pineal gland like a small flashlight
though
        not really strong enough—

I shift to the backstroke . . . body limp—what do I believe any-
more?
        *exhaustion is the opposite of wisdom . . .*

# Out Of the Pool

a thousand miles from salt spring island
your back/stroke has prevailed . . . as if the sky—
both day and night—
would have you for itself—

"*out of the pool time's up!*" whose voice is this
in the middle of empty blue? not a fist of rock in sight
not a ship / craft or vessel—
a mocking moon perhaps but only when full
whatever is the aether
shows no mercy to a mid-ocean pilgrim
"*out of the pool time's up!*" the imperative
falls out of the clouds
loud enough to be a god—echoes drifting
on the lightest winds

but I plug my ears . . . in time there will be
*nothing* left to swim through—does aether
then claim its *ethereal* victim?
song without body
lighter than air?

## Wherever She Wanders . . .

forward *Psyche* goes
                    always forward
as though *time*
was that colloquial 'river'
and the
brightest rapids
flared far ahead—

luminous
through chalky poplars
river bends
then steppes    high
walls narrowing
but always forward:
        even to
                    displease a god

# The Holding Tank

I never found the crone at sea . . . but traces appeared in many
places:  poems on rough hulls   beached or overturned in
shallows—dispirited   exhausted
                    I now think this ocean a holding tank—

                    and the primary question remains: where
do we go when the flesh disappears?   when
the crabs have had their fill?

is Okeanos a wading pool
                                for some elemental stage
                                        before
                                                deeper change?
            epiphanies at sea are contradictory—
                                unreliable
                                unverifiable

but once launched there is no turning back—
            "*poetry is ceremonial*" the crone
                    once said—floating is ritual
                                swimming is liturgy—
each stroke of the arms
            like a letter
                                on some vellum page

## Now We Go

she murmurs under the waves
we go like clouds
            in a crimson sunset—
salmon in sky
            salmon in sea
laughter rippling
            the crests and troughs
always another horizon /
always another sea / yet you
will never need to walk again
                        she whispers

you will fly or swim—one
and the same—but having killed
so much   in your
            eagerness to climb
you will never be given
            a second chance—
and now we go!  she cries
over the swells
            legless   weightless /
                  clouds in a saffron sky

## Author Note

In *Man Reading "Woman Reading in Bath"*, I have attempted to create a series of poetic meditations that respond to the work of Anne Szumigalski: specifically the poem entitled "Woman Reading in Bath", in the book that bares the same name. My inspiration was a statement made by this elder poet several times in her last few years: "Why do so many of my book titles have water in them?" At the time of her death, she was actually thinking about a play that would be performed in a swimming pool, with all rising and falling action found in the element in which she felt most comfortable. For me, the poem "Woman Reading in Bath" reflects a number of major themes in her work, and by writing individual poems in relation to single lines (occasionally a couplet), the 'mytho/poesis' of her work can be explicated; furthermore, the direction and spirit of her highly imaginative language can be rekindled though certainly not equalled.

Within this textual framework, these poems are dominated by metaphors of a swimmer enveloped in a series of states and environments. It would be understatement to say that these poems deal with loneliness, aloneness, and that final threshold state one experiences between life and death. The swimmer is a lonely human, but she/he accepts it as part of the rite of passage all mortals must make: moving from solid ground and social inclusion, to the beach with its visionary views, and finally the stage when one actually enters the water and moves out into a seemingly infinite ocean, beneath a tangibly eternal sky. Reflecting Szumigalski's own preoccupations with what she called the "Bigs and the Littles", the poems are continuously moving from microcosm to macrocosm, with the miraculous human body in the middle: the body that is itself sixty-five percent water, and that is formed in a placental womb/sea, and with the foetus that has gills and tail. But this soul/mind struggling with aloneness, trapped in a body endlessly swimming, is no light conceit for the play of metaphysical abstractions. It is in this dialectic of microcosm and macrocosm that I hope to personalize mystical and existential themes: at that level can be found a desolate man treading in the bays around Vancouver, in Georgia Strait, and about the shores of Salt Spring Island (my place of birth). Out of necessity, the swimmer is isolated from human society — he has taken that final plunge in search of an Absolute, if such an entity is possible (Anne liked the term Pleroma), and in the middle of the Pacific there are few signs to follow in search of ultimate union. But he does occasionally encounter signs of Szumigalski, who has preceded him into the unknown, and this reaffirms the notion of a possible way to higher being and healing. Exhausted, he is isolated from society and from the familiar God of the They; but a series of mammalian encounters — such as dolphins holding him afloat when he can no longer swim — offer hope and rest, allowing him to continue drifting on the "liquid mirrors of sky" that offer ineffable hues of the Holy.

One of the main reasons I chose this poem of Szumigalski's is its radical, though humorous, deconstruction of Patriarchal theologies. As suggested by the poem's title, there is a woman having a nice soak in the tub, but wouldn't you know it — a Yahweh-like figure pops out of the water and starts throwing his weight around. The woman is frightened at first and almost strangled by "tendrils" from his beard, but she manages to escape and look on as the Omnipotent Father, clearly too old for the job, begins to crumble into pieces. By the end of the poem a different, more inclusive, theology has emerged — one much kinder to the Body, the Earth, and particularly the Feminine. It is in my response to narrow theological concepts that the poems move into a specific duel with the hegemony of Patriarchal Christianity, and tries to show that the Gospel is ineffectual without the Feminine: was not Sofia, Wisdom, there at the side of God when He created the universe? Why would we exclude her now?

At times, my visions may seem Kafkaesque — as when the swimmer finds his eyes on one side of his face, becoming a flounder, and poses questions about the body in space. Other times there is a use of repetition that both breaks down and rebuilds the element water, the pelagic atmosphere, the death/dehydration of the body, and the role of God in nature. From the personal to the universal, this collection is an ode to the harmonics of mind, body, and spirit: why is the life journey most often compared to a river heading to the sea? Characters and Selves within all of us beg to know, the swimmer replies: the body is sixty-five percent H2O; the water breaks at birth and the babe is exiled to air; and in the unconscious process of Individuation, we are "drowning into life". In the end, I am simply expanding on Anne's question, "Why do so many of my titles include the word water?"

Anne Szumigalski and John Livingstone Clark